GUNS N'ROSES

C000242138

GUNS N' ROSES

THE WORLD'S MOST OUTRAGEOUS HARD ROCK BAND

PAUL ELLIOTT

HAMLYN

Acknowledgement: some source material has previously appeared in Sounds,
Kerrang!, RIP, RAW, Rolling Stone and Music Connection –
Paul Elliott.

Acknowledgments

The publishers would like to thank the following
organisations and individuals for their kind permission
to reproduce the photographs in this book:

All photographs by Ian Tilton except for the following:

Greg Freeman 10,11,17,18,19 1,30,31 t.1,31 b.1,31 b.r,32 t,
32 b.1,46 t.r,46 b.r,80

Tim Jarvis 36 t.r,36 b.1,36 b.r,37 b.1,37 t.1,37 t.r,37 b.r

L.F.I/Lynn McAfee 13,/Ilpo Musto 36 t.1,/Sam Hain 44–45

Pictorial Press/J. Mayer 8,/Bob Lease 12

Relay Photos 24,28,34 b,66 b,73,75,76/Justin Thomas 9,34 t,
41 t.1,44 1,58 main,70–71/Jon Conrad 16/Jodi Summers
26–27,72 b,/Alex Solca 41 b.r,/Gene Ambo 56,/David
Wainwright 62 b.1,65 main,/Paul Natkin 2–3,72,77

Retna Pictures Ltd./Larry Busacca 25,32 b.r,46 t.1,/
Eddie Malluk 28 b,58 b.r,68 main/Jennifer Rose 57 main,/
Y.Moto 61 main/Tony Mottram 63

Rex Features Ltd., 33,35,45

Published in 1990
by The Hamlyn Publishing Group Limited
a division of The Octopus Publishing Group,
Michelin House, 81 Fulham Road, London SW3 6RB

Copyright © The Hamlyn Publishing Group Limited 1990

All rights reserved. No part of this publication
may be reproduced, stored in a retrieval system,
or transmitted in any form or by any means,
electronic, mechanical, photocopying, recording
or otherwise, without the permission of
the copyright holders.

ISBN 0 600 56796 6

Printed in Great Britain

CONTENTS

INTRODUCTION

Guns N' Roses are one of the biggest-selling rock 'n' roll bands on the planet these days, but they're still the same street trash they always were.

Steven's still crazy, Duff's still cool, Izzy's still fazed, Slash is still drunk, Axl's still one bad mother. They're still wild, still louder than hell, still the meanest, rawest rock band in America.

No amount of royalty money could ever make Guns N' Roses clean. Their music will always carry the stink of gasoline alley.

Guns came out of Hollywood in 1987, sweating decadence. Each had ghosted into Los Angeles from Nowhere, USA. Rock 'n' roll is their salvation, their life. They live it hard and fast.

What you're holding is a fly-on-the-wall life history of the most sensational and controversial rock 'n' roll band since the Sex Pistols. Their story ain't pretty. It is rock 'n' roll Babylon personified.

Sex, drugs, violence, here is the shocking truth, from the band's own lips. Follow Guns N' Roses from The Whiskey A Go Go in Los Angeles to the Marquee in London; from Manchester to Dallas and back to Donington from sticky-walled whiskey holes to cowshed coliseums. Taste the reckless life of the road; the sweat, the triumphs, the heartbreak, the excess.

See Guns grow from Hollywood

Paul Elliott.

brats into the people's rock 'n' roll band of the late '80s and '90s.

Guns N' Roses are misfits who've caught the mood of the world's restless, estranged youth. Kids picking up guitars want to spit in society's face like Guns N' Roses do.

This band bleeds for its music like no other. Guns N' Roses are the ultimate rock outlaws.

Here is an eye witness account of the birth of a rock 'n' roll legend.

RAISING HELL
IN THE CITY OF ANGELS

The Whiskey A Go Go, Hollywood, Los Angeles, California. 16 March 1987.

Five punks, all rag and bone and psyched stares, spill on to a stage the size of a beer crate. The air is dry and charged, the joint heaving. The guest list would stretch halfway down Sunset Boulevard but few have come just to hang out and drain the bar. Rubber and leather groans as toes arch and necks strain for a clear sight of LA's newest kings of the gutter.

"Guns," bawls a roadie compère, "N' Fuckin' Roses!!"

The intro tape is 'What's That Noise?' by SOD (Stormtroopers of Death). As it spits and misfires its 57 seconds of hardcore chaos, guitar hands claw up, knuckles whiten. The tape cuts, drummer Steven Adler beats a frenzied cue and the guitars come down hard. They gun 'Reckless Life', hot metal and methedrine.

The lip of the stage is suddenly a blur of headstocks and dripping hair. Limbs thrash and sweat rains. The music kicks and screams.

Steven's blond mane is soon dark with fluid. Shirtless, he works a streamlined kit, quick hands whipping hard. He smiles, alone.

W. Axl Rose, shadowed by Izzy Stradlin' (*left*); Duff McKagan (*right*). Beer drinkers and hell raisers. Vagabonds of the western world.

Axl, tattooed
beat messiah,
on stage at The
Whiskey A Go Go,
Hollywood, USA.

Duff McKagan greases the rhythm with a bass tugged from down around his boots. Tall, lean, Duff moves with a slow sway that's half lazy, half boozy. Under straggles of dirty gold and black, his seems the coolest head in Guns N' Roses.

As scruffy and heavy-lidded as the average big-city wino, Izzy Stradlin' prowls the shadows. He hugs the backline, throttling a big white Gibson and sucking on a chain of cigarettes which he chews into spent ash in seconds. When the riffs turn nasty – stinging like the Sex Pistols on 'It's So Easy' – Izzy's lips curl, teeth clench, his expression sour and intense.

Stage right is Slash, looking like the Ramone that time forgot. Booze brudder. Stripped to the waist. Dark ringlets in his eyes. Head bowed and reeling with the stink of whiskey.

He opens his shoulders and lets his head roll back; seemingly frazzled beyond help, yet his coal-black Les Paul lashes with a tongue like a razor, leads bleeding rage, danger, melancholy.

Alongside coppertan Slash, W Axl Rose seems pale, spectral. He wears just supple purple leather pants sunk into tatty cowboy boots. China-white skin stretches across his ribcage and appears thin, almost to the point of translucence.

As 'Welcome To The Jungle' coils and rumbles, Axl melts into the shape of the crucifix hung about his neck. His sinewy arms spread, knotted with veins and blue with tattoos.

Spittle wells in the sharp corners of his mouth and jets out with the poison of his words.

The poetry he spins is black and bitter with the shit of the city, clammy with sex, haunted by death. Shadowboxing and sidewinding, his movements are mesmeric.

The legendary Whiskey A Go Go smacks of girls and liquor but tonight's thrill is live naked rock 'n' roll. Guns N' Roses are pissing raw depravity up the club's clean brick-face walls.

Saw-toothed riffs recall the greatest gut rock. AC/DC, Aerosmith, the Rolling Stones, Sex Pistols, Led Zeppelin, Hanoi Rocks. A shrieky, spluttering sound mix rattles but can't jam their motor.

"Ain't my fault the PA sucks!" spits Axl; which is as near as this band gets to apologising.

Feeding off wild adrenalin and whatever else comes to hand, Guns N' Roses rip and tear through the meat of their soon-to-be-released debut album *Appetite For Destruction*. 'You're Crazy', 'Nightrain', 'My

Slash with the devil's right hand, the Gibson Les Paul.

Michelle'. Bullets from a misfit's heart, anthems to the estranged.

The set comes to a violent end, they shoot surly thanks and exit. Guns N' Roses quit the Whiskey having proved themselves the most intoxicating hard rock 'n' roll band in the world.

Two road years later, Guns return to Los Angeles as the people's rock 'n' roll band of the late Eighties and early Nineties.

LA GUNS 'N' HOLLYWOOD ROSES

WAxl Rose, Izzy Stradlin', Duff McKagan, Steven Adler and Slash played their first gig together as Guns N' Roses at The Troubadour, a smallish club in Los Angeles.

"It was a Thursday night," says Slash. "I'd rehearsed with the band for two days."

"As of June '85," adds Axl, "*this* was Guns N' Roses."

Individually, the band give confused accounts of the events leading up to that legendary Thursday night. The past is perhaps blurred by too much Night Train.

The original Guns N' Roses featured Axl, Izzy, Duff, Rob Gardner and Tracii Guns. It was early '85. Axl and Izzy had been in LA for three years, sleeping rough. Duff was fresh out of Seattle.

The name Guns N' Roses was a hybrid of LA Guns and Hollywood Roses, two bands in which various members were involved. Before settling on GN'R, they'd dreamt up a string of bizarre names, including AIDS and Heads Of Amazon.

When, in May of '85, Rob and Tracii dragged their feet at the prospect of a club tour that Duff had set up along the West Coast, Slash and Steven were called up at Duff's suggestion. Slash and Steven were the existing two-man nucleus of a spluttering local band, Road Crew, which Duff had spent a short time playing bass for.

Exit Rob and Tracii, the latter to reform LA Guns.

Strangely, Axl refers in an early interview to playing a gig "with Slash and Steve in Hollywood Rose," a band which the other two fail to mention. In addition, Duff claims that it was he who "told Axl about Slash and Steven."

Even the chronology is muddled. If Slash and Steven were drafted for a West Coast tour, was the Troubadour debut simply a warm-up show? Only Guns N' Roses themselves

Guns N' Roses; an early study. Just another day in Paradise City.

know the answers to these mysteries. And they can't remember!

Perversely, they each have total recall of their squalid early communal band lifestyle. The big neon glitz of Los Angeles had sucked them in like flies and, as Izzy succinctly puts it, "we had to eat shit to get where we are!"

Before signing to Geffen, Guns N' Roses lived hand-to-mouth.

"We tried to live on $3.75 a day," reveals Axl, "which was enough to buy biscuits and gravy at Denny's for a buck and a quarter, a bottle of Night Train for a buck and a quarter, or some really cheap wine like Thunderbird. That's it. We survived. Even if you were dead tired you made a party."

All five of the band slept wherever they could in a ramshackle studio

"That's it. We survived. Even if you were dead tired you made a party."

apartment in Hollywood. It was dubbed The Hellhouse, "but God," beams Slash, "did we sound good in there!"

"We tried to get as many girls into the loft as we could. I don't know. It got pretty wild. There was a lot of indoor and outdoor sex. We were living there when we got signed and every one of us was broke at the time."

The band also lived for a short time at the West Hollywood apartment of their first manager, Vicky Hamilton. Into one large room they crammed amps, guitars, clothes, bodies, any old rubbish. Vicky had recently helped put Poison's cheap glam cabaret into America's stadia.

"She doesn't get to pay her rent," said Slash at the time, "'cause she spends all the money she can possibly get her hands on trying to get us off the ground."

The band's sole means of support was, Steven laughs, "G.I.R.L.S."

"We sold drugs," drawls Izzy, "sold girls. We *managed*. In the beginning we'd throw parties and ransack the girl's purse while one of the guys was with her."

"Not being sexist or anything," adds Slash, clumsily, "it's fucking amazing how much abuse girls will take! At one point, most of us had girlfriends, but as soon as the band started happening – goodbye.

"It didn't have a shower," continues Axl. "And the rain always leaked in. I once stole this wood and we built this loft so we could have a place to sleep above our equipment. We tried to get as many girls into the loft as we could. I don't know. It got pretty wild. There was a lot of indoor and outdoor sex. We were living there when we got signed and every one of us was broke at the time."

They're a pain in the ass. They take up too much time and they have their own ideas which they're constantly throwing in your face."

"At that point in my career it was easier for me not to have a girlfriend," reasons Axl. "Besides, I didn't have the money to support a girlfriend. And they got tired of having to take you to dinner every day."

"We love to take care of women," insists Steve, "we love to treat them great. But we didn't have any money then, so we treated 'em like shit."

Guns N' Roses played LA's notorious dives – The Whiskey, The Roxy, The Troubadour, Scream.

"Their draw," explained Vicky back in '86, "went from 150 to 700 almost overnight. I think it was their friends networking more than anything. It was word-of-mouth, not advertising.

Says Axl: "As soon as we began headlining we brought in different opening bands like Jetboy, Faster Pussycat and LA Guns, and it kinda created this scene. In that crowd we were pretty much the top draw.

"She doesn't get to pay her rent," said Slash at the time, "'cause she spends all the money she can possibly get her hands on trying to get us off the ground."

Izzy in the hungry years.

bands out. We always tried to help others 'cause I wanna see a really cool rock scene. I wanna be able to turn on my radio and not be sick about the shit I'm gonna hear."

"The thought of the LA scene just made me sick," sneers Slash. "LA is considered a pretty gay place and we got a lotta flak from people thinkin' we were posers."

"Poison fucked it up for all of us," griped Axl. "They said that everyone in LA was following *their* trend! I've told those guys personally that they can lock me in a room with all of them and I'll be the only one who walks out!"

Having flirted for months on end with several record companies as a means of dining out for free, Guns N' Roses finally signed to Geffen Records on 25 March 1986. Soon after, Guns split with Vicky Hamilton.

Tom Zutaut and Teresa Ensenat, the A&R team who'd procured Guns N' Roses for Geffen, then spent several frantic months seeking out a new manager for the band. Zutaut brought Aerosmith manager Tim Collins to LA for a showcase gig. Afterwards, the band ran up a 400-dollar drinks tab on Collins' hotel bill when he'd checked into a second room in order to get some sleep. By the morning, Collins decided he'd seen enough.

In August Englishman Alan Niven was hired as Guns N' Roses manager. At that point $100,000 had been spent on recording for the band's first album and there was no usable material in the can. Niven, so the legend on *Appetite For Destruction*'s inner sleeve goes, came in and kicked ass when it was needed.

Eventually, we quit playing for a while to work on the record *Appetite For Destruction* and the others started headlining, but some of them weren't as cool about helping other

W. AXL ROSE

Rock outlaw archetype. Bleeding heart romantic. Jail-bird. Desperado. Loner. Manic depressive. Junk fiend. One bad, dog-slayin' mother. Dirt with an angel face. A brawler. A bigot. A corpse.

Rumour has nailed W Axl Rose as amoral, schizoid, petulant, out of control, even dead. Axl's not dead. He shot a pig, not a whole pack of dogs. But there is a core of truth amid the other rumours, given that each story is inevitably fleshed out with a little cheap sensationalism.

"Axl," joked Slash back in 1986, "is just another version of The Ayatollah!"

It's a lazy, throwaway caricature, but it says something of Axl's fire and will to lead.

Guns N' Roses' uncompromising vocalist has followed his own heart and stubborn convictions from an early age. Born 6 February 1962 in Lafayette, Indiana, he was raised as Bill Bailey, eldest son of L. Stephen and Sharon Bailey.

Aged 17 and bored of smalltown mid-America, Bill began wearing his red-bronze hair long, singing in local garage bands, clashing with his parents.

He was all mouth, angst and spunk when he suddenly discovered his hitherto secret past. L. Stephen Bailey was in fact his stepfather. His surname at birth was indeed Rose, and his natural father – a wrecker and rolling stone, whose current whereabouts are unknown – upped and left Sharon when Bill was little more than a babe-in-arms.

Bill exploded with confused anger. He re-christened himself W Rose and his frustrations were expressed in a classic case history of juvenile delinquency. Adding to his new name that of Axl, a band in which he had sung, Rose was soon familiar with the Lafayette police cells.

"I got thrown in jail over 20 times," he recalls bitterly, "and five of those times I was guilty. Of what? Public consumption – I was drinking at a party under-age. The other times I got busted 'cos the cops hated me. So I don't have much love for that fucking place!"

Now less angry than before, Axl regards his stepfather as his "real dad". Nevertheless, he legally changed his name to W Axl Rose shortly before Guns N' Roses signed their recording contract with the Geffen label in March of 1986.

"Axl," joked Slash back in 1986, "is just another version of The Ayatollah!"

Axl possesses at least "five or six different voices". His temperament is equally volatile.

Psychiatrists have clinically diagnosed his condition as a manic-depressive disorder, which is prevalent among individuals of exceptional ability. Axl struggles to contain his "mood swings" with the aid of Lithium.

"I'm very sensitive and emotional. Things upset me and make me feel like not functioning or dealing with people, the band or anything.

"I went to a clinic thinking it would help my moods. The only thing I did was take one 500-question test — y'know, filling in all the little black dots. All of a sudden I'm diagnosed manic-depressive!

"'Let's put Axl on medication'. Well, the medication doesn't help me deal with stress. The only thing it does is

W. Axl Rose. One bad mother.

help keep people off my back because they figure I'm on medication."

Axl's psychosis was also noted back in Indiana by a close friend, Jeff Isabelle; another of Lafayette's wild ones, now better known as Izzy Stradlin'.

"He was a serious lunatic when I met him," remembers Izzy, "really fucking bent on fighting and destroying things."

As Izzy sees it, rock 'n' roll, specifically Guns N' Roses, is Axl's salvation.

"If it wasn't for the band, I just hate to think what he'd have done."

"I go crazy," Axl confesses. "I clear a club if an argument starts. Slash has a way of working things out a bit and avoiding trouble as much as possible. He seems to slip into corners and he doesn't know how he does it. *I'm* right in someone's face saying, 'What do you *mean* we can't have more beer?'"

The flipside to this bilious and self-destructive aggression is the quiet intensity which is mirrored in the simple, soul-baring romanticism of 'Patience' or 'Sweet Child O' Mine'. Axl is a great conversationalist. After shows, he'll talk till past sunrise with assorted hangers-on, or he'll just slip away quietly and lock himself behind that night's hotel room door.

Before the band's success sky-rocketed, it was principally Axl who harangued the world's press with the hardline according to Guns N' Roses. He's a sharp and garrulous interviewee, his voice soft, deep, slightly rasping, his hands a flurry of gestures. Now, misquoted and misinterpreted, he rarely opens up to the media.

It's from a stage that he can truly communicate.

"I live for the songs. If I go through a bad time, well, anything I have to go through is worth it if I've got a song out of it."

"If I had to sleep in a parking garage and hated it but got a song out of the experience, I'm glad that I had to go through a ton of shit – I've got a bitchin' song."

"When I'm onstage, that's when I get to take what I'm worth to the public. When I'm singing a line, I'm thinking of the feelings that made me come up with the song in the first place. At the same time, I think about how I feel singing those words now, and how those words are gonna hit people in the crowd.

"I usually have to have someone stand beside me when I come off stage because I can't really even tie my own shoes, I've gone through so many thoughts on stage."

Pre-album Los Angeles club shows were especially fraught.

"You look out at a crowd of 700 people and you know 300 of them. This person loves you, this one hates you and this one's mad at you because you owe him five bucks and you're mad at another guy 'cause he owes you 25."

"You see all this stuff, plus you're thinking about the feelings in the music. I try to put every single thought I possibly can into every performance and every line. And that's why I might be known as histrionic, 'cause I go full out."

Dallas 1988. The band offstage and on.

"If you're bored of a song and it's one of your songs, you just play it. It's like having a pair of pants. Those pants meant something to you at one time – you liked 'em or whatever – but you just outgrow 'em, you're tired of wearing them, and they're not you anymore. Some songs I rewrite 'cause the verses aren't me anymore.

"I can come off the stage in tears because I was so moved by the music. I want people to feel that too.

"In my life as a singer there have been a few times when I've gone into a trance while I'm singing and have come to as if I'd been knocked out on the floor, because I was so far into the song. There's been a couple of times while singing 'You're Crazy' when I've got lost in the song and then found I was almost ready to fall off the stage! I try to throw myself into the song that much every time. I really don't feel like I'm breaking free of my emotions. I feel like I'm trying to."

As Bill Bailey and as W Axl Rose, life has been a struggle for self-expression. Broken hearts, busted jaws; it's all inspiration.

"I explore emotional situations of any kind – with a lover, a friend – and try to put it into the best words I can. Something good or tragic, something that moves me so much that my mind can't seem to escape."

When Guns N' Roses toured America with Aerosmith in the summer of 1989, fevered reports of Axl's alleged death circulated at the rate of at least one per week. The craziest story claimed that Slash had shot the singer dead!

Slash and firearms are the least of Axl's worries. Two weeks prior to Guns N' Roses first UK shows at London's Marquee club in June 1987, Axl lay under electrodes in a Los Angeles hospital's intensive care unit. Yes, it was that close.

Axl is reckless, but where Izzy and Slash sank body and soul into the hell of heroin addiction, Axl never lost control.

A high-IQ hellraiser with a liver of granite and a bruised rock 'n' roll heart on his sleeve, Axl is strong, sensitive too, but wildly unpredictable, even to those he's lived, loved and worked with for years.

"He can still be a tyrant," admits Izzy, "but then he can turn around and be the nicest guy in the world."

'He does a lotta weird shit that no-one understands," shrugs Slash, "But I love the guy. He's a sweetheart, and the most temperamental fucking meanest little fuck in the world!"

ANOTHER ROCK 'N' ROLL SUICIDE

" **I** don't care if you think I've got a bad attitude or if I'm being big-headed about it," blurted Slash back in '86, "This is the only rock 'n' roll band to come out of LA that's real and the kids know it."

"They haven't seen anything like it in the last ten years," concludes Axl. "Van Halen was the last real rock 'n' roll band out of LA."

"Mötley Crüe was more teen-metal," decides Izzy. "We go for a more roots-oriented sound."

Guns N' Roses first came to wide-

"This is the only rock 'n' roll band to come out of LA that's real and the kids know it."

spread notoriety in 1986 with the release of their first EP, *Live ?!*@ *Like A Suicide*, a four-tracker issued on their own Uzi Suicide label. *Suicide* brought to the world Guns N'

Roses live, ragged, uncensored. The band were declared natural successors to the legendary Aerosmith, who stood for 15 years as the definitive American rock 'n' roll band. The connection was inevitable given that *Suicide* numbered amongst its tracks a cover of Aerosmith's 'Mama Kin'.

"In my mind," said Axl, "the hardest, ballsiest rock band that ever came out of America was Aerosmith. What I always liked about 'em was that they weren't the guys you'd want to meet at the end of an alley if you'd had a disagreement. I always wanted to come out of America with that same attitude.

"So, one reason why there's been this Aerosmith comparison is, fuck, they were the only goddam role model to come out of here! They were a tradition that I grew up with. They were the only band that people who lived in my city in Indiana would accept wearing make-up and dressing cool. These people thought the Stones were fags, but everybody liked Aerosmith. We are influenced by them but it goes deeper than that in that we're also influenced by some of the things they're influenced by, like Muddy Waters, Howlin' Wolf, old blues things, black artists."

Less flatteringly, Guns N' Roses

were frequently dismissed as just another year's model of the perennial badass LA crotch-rock band.

Argued Slash: "The only reason we get that bad-boy shit is because the other bands in LA are such wimps!"

GN'R were even tarred 'glam', no doubt as a reference to the kitsch scarves worn by Steven and Slash in the EP's rear sleeve photograph.

"We don' know what glam is," sulked Izzy at the time.

"Glam," spat Axl, "reminds me of bands like Angel who rely more on fashion than their music."

"If I had to label this band," grumbled Slash, "I'd say that it's a hard rock band with an R&B base. It's not a glam band, not a heavy metal band, not a country band."

"We listen to funk, disco, metal, classical," explained Axl. "We listen to soundtracks, old Fifties stuff, Sixties music."

"We're influenced by all of it. We're not doing anything that I would call original, it's all been done before."

"We're not doing anything new — we're just trying to be as sincere as we can with our music and just put it out the best way we can. In other words, all our songs ain't gonna be mellow, they're gonna have a heavy edge to them."

Live ?!@ *Like A Suicide* mixes two cover versions with two GN'R originals. The second is a frenetic run through Rose Tattoo's 'Nice Boys', a cut from the now-defunct Australian quintet's *Rock 'N' Roll Outlaws*.

The original songs are seedy autobiographies: 'Reckless Life' ("it's my only vice"), born of arrogant, masochistic abandon, and 'Move To The City', straight from Izzy and Axl's gypsy hearts. Guns N' Roses dedicated *Suicide* "to all the people who have helped keep us alive"; "to our friends," according to the sleeve, "for support in the streets as well as the stage."

Explained Izzy: "We felt that all the people who saw us from the beginning should have a chance to get our early stuff on record. So we only printed up 10,000 copies. That way, they can feel they have a special limited edition. It's like an expensive dedication to all the kids who helped us get going when we had no money."

The EP also served as a stop-gap. When *Suicide* hit the streets, *Appetite For Destruction* was recorded and mixed but wasn't due for release for another six months.

STEVEN ADLER

"I'm from Hollywood. Born and raised in America."

Steven Adler was born 22 January 1965 in Cleveland, Ohio, but is the living, breathing essence of California. Sun-dried ash blond, tanned, slim, blue-eyed and carefree. Steven was a teenage Kiss freak and is in many ways still the same easygoing and purely hedonistic beach bum who at 15 got Slash hip to the electric guitar.

Drums were not Steven's first love but when, at around 17, he figured his guitar playing wasn't working out so well, he took to beating on pots and pans and saving for a full-blown drum kit. At one point, fearing he'd never scrape together enough money, Steven hit on the idea of singing. Briefly and without success, he fronted one of many low-key Hollywood garage bands that Slash was working on.

Stung by failure, Steven quit singing and got back to the serious business of playing drums. Slash was in a band named Road Crew – "the first real musical thing I had that actually went out and played at high schools and parties" – when all of a sudden, the guitarist remembers:

"Steven showed up one day and said, 'Get rid of your drummer, he's not good enough.'"

Steven had somehow got his hands on a kit and he'd gotten good. Me and Steven carried Road Crew on, which was a great little band. Sorta like what Metallica are now without a singer."

Steven's drumming is direct and sweats hard, dispensing with flash and frills. Likewise, he's portrayed by those around him as an exuberant personality, big-hearted and of simple tastes. In the industry's working vernacular, Steven lives to play rock 'n' roll and get his dick sucked.

An early interview, printed in a Los Angeles-based periodical prior to the band signing to Geffen, asked each of Guns N' Roses to name their one greatest wish.

Steven Adler, aka Mr. Lewis Cipher: I was a teenage Kiss freak.

Slash craved "a constant supply of Marlboros," Izzy a "Maserati four-wheel drive." Duff wished the first record was released and the band were out on the road. Axl, difficult again, wanted "all the wishes there are to have." Steven simply sought "peace of mind."

Amid the madness of a megabuck rock 'n' roll tour, Steven could hardly be more relaxed. Before a show at a sold-out 15,000-capacity Texan arena, he saunters about the dressing room, idly talking and laughing, rattling his sticks on flightcases and slurping down vials of syrupy royal jelly. "Builds up come in your balls!" he gurgles.

Steven. A born celebrity.

Diary of a road hog.

Steven Adler is a born celebrity. He gets a kick out of the star trip but deals with the glitz and the hubbub on the most straightforward level. He loves to sign autographs and just hasn't the heart to say no to an on-stage jam; more recently, he goofed off with Bon Jovi in San Diego.

Given the popular assumption that people who hit things for a living are inevitably weak of mind, Steven has been branded shallow by some who've come into brief contact with him. While this may be a consequence of his boyish sense of fun, it's also apparent that the media generally hang on a singer's every word while dismissing those of a drummer as mere small talk.

This isn't so. Off the cuff, Steven crystallises the Los Angeles bullshit rock society in a single sentence.

"In LA, there's a million people who think they're musicians and only a few who are."

During breaks in touring Steven rehearses and refines new material mainly with Duff and Slash. And on 3 June 1989, he wed his longtime girlfriend Cheryl in Las Vegas.

However, it's on the road that Steven, like Slash, feels truly at ease. His appetite for touring is such that he even asked manager Alan Niven if he could roadie for another of Niven's charges, Great White, as a means of getting back out on the open road.

Known to hotels the world over as Mr Lewis Cipher, Steven Adler is a certifiable road hog with an itch that two solid years of touring couldn't scratch. He and Slash will never be genuinely happy unless there's a new album in the stores and Guns N' Roses are riding out the road and air miles on sweat and adrenalin.

SEEDS OF DESTRUCTION

In the Spring of 1987, Guns N' Roses had left The Hellhouse and were receiving their routine LAPD calls at a new band residence – a smallish, beat-up wooden bungalow off Santa Monica Boulevard, its white paintwork flaking, its driveway and lawn overflowing with both working and rotting automobiles.

Amid shabby furniture, piles of clothes, guitars, speaker cabs and sacks of garbage lay the seeds of destruction, the scratchy old records that fired the band's collective imagination. Plenty of Rolling Stones, Aerosmith, Sex Pistols, Metallica, Ramones, Misfits, Queen, Led Zeppelin, AC/DC, Bo Diddley.

"In one year I spent over 1300 dollars on cassettes, everything from Slayer to Wham!, to listen to production, vocals, melodies, this and that," reveals Axl. "I'm from Indiana where Lynyrd Skynyrd are considered God to the point that you end up saying, I hate this fucking band! And yet for our song 'Sweet Child O' Mine' I went out and got some old Lynyrd Skynyrd tapes to make sure that we'd got that downhome, heartfelt feeling."

Appetite For Destruction was released worldwide on 31 July 1987.

> "In one year I spent over 1300 dollars on cassettes, everything from Slayer to Wham!"

When hired, producer Mike Clink wasn't a big name, but the last thing Guns N' Roses needed was a prima donna at the mixing desk. Clink had two qualifications: "great guitar sounds and a tremendous amount of patience." His brief was to transfer to flat tape all the new emotion that had burned inside the members of Guns N' Roses for 20, 25 years. He got it all: rage, paranoia, lust, spite, love.

Like 'Move To The City' before it, 'Welcome To The Jungle' shivers with the cold sweat of a country boy cut loose in the big city. In the promo video, Axl plays the saucer-eyed hick, Izzy the great shark. 'Out Ta Get Me', dedicated at the Marquee to the band's critics, blows up

Los Angeles, March 1987. The killer rock 'n' roll album of the 1980s is fresh in the can.

in the face of the Indiana and Los Angeles police; "The West Hollywood sheriffs," remarked a weary Izzy upon the album's release, "have gotta be the biggest fucking pig-faces I've ever known!"

'Nightrain' glorifies GN'R's favourite cheap killer wine – "you drink a quarter," says Axl, "and you black out" – while 'Mr Brownstone' tells the inside story on heroin addiction. Says Slash: "There was a point where I stopped playing guitar and didn't even talk to my band, except for Izzy, 'cause we were both doing it. I didn't come out of my apartment for three months, except to go to the market. The one thing that really stopped me was a phone call from Duff, saying, 'You've alienated yourself from everybody'. Since they're the only people I'm really close to, that really affected me, and I quit."

"I didn't come out of my apartment for three months, except to go to the market."

'Sweet Child O'Mine' was written for Axl's girlfriend Erin, daughter of Everly Brother Don. 'Rocket Queen' and 'My Michelle' are also real life stories of girls whom Axl has known.

"When I first wrote 'My Michelle'," remembers Axl. "I'd written it all nice and I thought, that's not how it really is. So I wrote the real story down, kind of as a joke. She and her dad ended up loving it. It's a true story – I met her when I was 13 and went out with her later – and that's what works, I think.

31

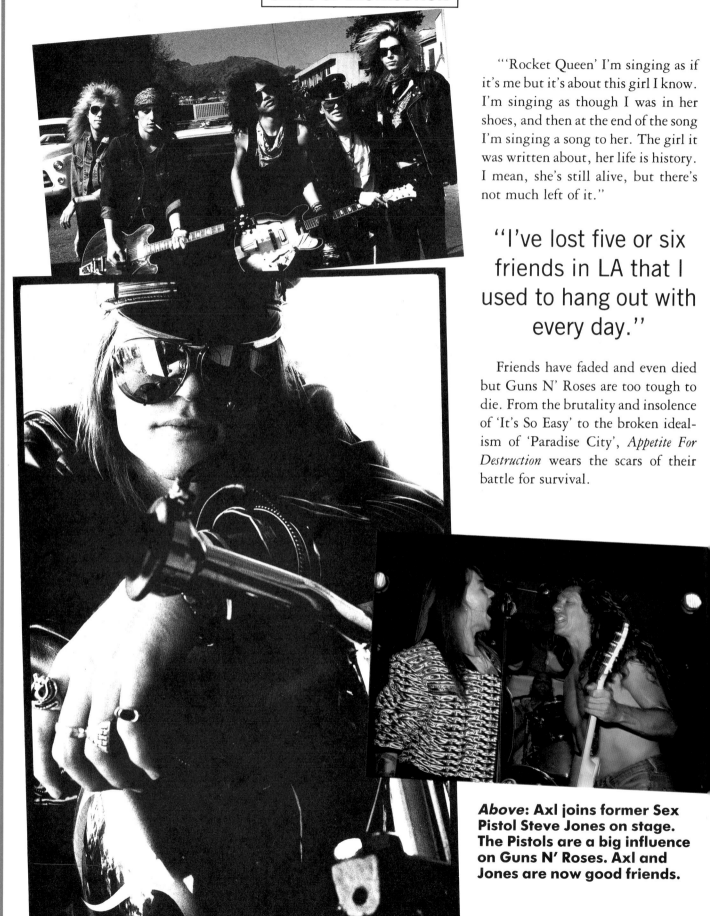

"'Rocket Queen' I'm singing as if it's me but it's about this girl I know. I'm singing as though I was in her shoes, and then at the end of the song I'm singing a song to her. The girl it was written about, her life is history. I mean, she's still alive, but there's not much left of it."

"I've lost five or six friends in LA that I used to hang out with every day."

Friends have faded and even died but Guns N' Roses are too tough to die. From the brutality and insolence of 'It's So Easy' to the broken idealism of 'Paradise City', *Appetite For Destruction* wears the scars of their battle for survival.

Above: Axl joins former Sex Pistol Steve Jones on stage. The Pistols are a big influence on Guns N' Roses. Axl and Jones are now good friends.

SUMMER IN SOHO

"It's good to be in fucking England finally," Axl half purrs, half hisses. Guns N' Roses can at last dig their heels into the stage of London's famous old Marquee club in Soho's Wardour Street.

But a bristling crowd isn't about to let LA's new big thing just roll into London unchallenged. Rattling through 'Reckless Life' and 'Out Ta Get Me', Guns N' Roses are met with a hail of plastic beerglasses. Phlegm from the first few rows sticks and hangs in Izzy and Axl's hair. Axl's hackles rise.

"Hey! If you wanna keep throwin' things we're gonna fuckin' leave! Whaddaya think?"

Another glass clatters into Steven's cymbals.

"Hey!" Axl boils. "Fuck you, pussy!"

The barrage slows to a trickle by the end of the third song, 'Anything Goes'. Guns N' Roses have won out.

The month which Guns N' Roses spent on the streets of London in the summer of '87 stank of controversy. They rode into Britain on a bad reputation; even on the Los Angeles–London flight, a drunk Slash all but burnt his own ass off slumbering in a

Guns N' Roses are met with a hail of plastic beerglasses. Phlegm from the first few rows sticks and hangs in Izzy and Axl's hair.

The Marquee, Soho, London; 19 June 1987.

Guns N' Roses doing it the hard way, the only way. The crowd at the Marquee put up a fight, but the Guns ain't quitters. June 19 was a bloody victory, one of many.

seat that he'd unwittingly set on fire with a cigarette!

"A rock band even nastier than the Beastie Boys is heading for Britain," quaked the *Star* newspaper. "Los Angeles-based Guns N' Roses are led by the outrageous Axl Rose, who has an endearing habit of butchering dogs. Record company bosses are already worried that Rose's hatred of dogs could cause a backlash amongst animal lovers. He is on record as saying: 'I have a personal disgust for small dogs, like poodles. Everything about them means I must kill them.' The other two [!] members of the group are as sleazy as their crackpot

leader. Guitarist Slash and bass player Duff McKagan claim they have been on a boozing binge for TWO YEARS. Says Slash: 'When we get up in the afternoon we can't play because our hands are shaking like windmills.'"

Axl was joking, Slash was exaggerating, but the reputation stuck. The *Star* also reported that in an

"I have a personal disgust for small dogs, like poodles. Everything about them means I must kill them."

earlier incident back on the West Coast, Axl had been hospitalised "for three days after a vicious battle with LA police." Axl himself gave a muddled account of the incident.

"It just kinda happened real quickly. I got hit on the head by a cop and I guess I just blacked out. Two days later I woke up in hospital tied to the bed with electrodes over

me. I guess they had to give me electro-shock. I don't know a whole lot about what happened."

Back then, the party was never over for Axl till police or paramedics rolled up. Had he not been admitted to hospital so quickly, Guns N' Roses might never have made it out of Los Angeles.

Trouble, it seemed, lurked at every corner. "Y'know," shrugged Axl at the first Marquee gig, "we just got here, right? I go to Tower Rec-

"Two days later I woke up in hospital tied to the bed with electrodes over me."

ords, I sit down, and the security throw me out. And then they call the local constables – ain't that what they call 'em? And they were a coupla right dickheads. They'll be getting

letters to their bosses, a nice little write-up."

Axl, accompanied by Alan Niven and Tom Zutaut of Geffen Records, had gone late one night to the Tower Records store at Piccadilly Circus. Drowsy with jet-lag and the side effects of an anti-histamine drug he'd taken to break up some congestion, Axl sat on a step in Tower's cassette department, where he had just bought an Eagles tape. Three large members of the store's security staff

allegedly pulled him up without first showing their ID. An ugly shouting match and the inevitable jostling ensued. Eventually the police were called to intervene.

"The cops are kinda different here," reflected Axl. "When they turned up at Tower, Alan [Niven] said to 'em, 'Take your hands off me!' And they did! Back in LA, they won't take any of that shit. You'd be slung straight across the front of the squad car with a gun to your head!"

Guns N' Roses played three shows at the Marquee – 19, 22 and 28 June – each one better than the last.

"The crowd were so fuckin' into it," Axl smiled. "So much energy. They threw some shit to start with but they cooled it after a while. But shit, it was hot in there! Real hard to breathe. Steven lost about ten pounds in weight during each show. I'd got out of hospital only a week before the first show. When we started that show it was like, man, we're in hell!"

Axl left London with some popular myths exploded – "English beer ain't that fuckin' warm!" – and others still a mystery: "what the fuck is

Spotted Dick? I can't believe you eat this thing called Spotted Dick!"

Guns N' Roses entered Britain with the reputation of sex-crazed, booze-sodden, drug-dealin' dog-killers. They left with a reputation as the most electrifying live rock 'n' roll band on the planet.

"D'ya like my shirt?" grinned Axl at the Marquee. "It says, 'Fuck Dancing, Let's Fuck!' I think that gets to the point!"

So had Guns N' Roses.

June 1987. Izzy and Slash hold up their weary, drunken frames for the British music press at the Soho offices of WEA Records, just a whisky bottle's throw from the Marquee.

SLASH

Two knocks at the door are followed by a thin voice.

"Message for Mr Peter Cottontail."

There are no cartoon rabbits in. Only an off-duty rock guitarist, wet from a shower, towel clinging to his waist, damp hair veiling his dark eyes and a large tumbler of Jack Daniel's in one hand. Slash peers round the door and takes the slip of paper from the bemused hotel porter.

He chuckles over another sleazy birthday greeting. Slash has just turned 23 – 'HAPPY FUCKIN' BIRTHDAY, YOU FUCKER!' spat the cake icing. It's Dallas, Texas, 23 July 1988. The gig is tomorrow night and Slash's liver and testicles are braced for a long, hard night of celebration.

Slash lives for the road.

"Ozzy Osborne is someone I can relate to," he explains. "His life is so rock 'n' roll oriented. He doesn't have anything else. That's the way I feel."

Slash was born Saul Hudson in Stoke-on-Trent, England, in 1965 ("Stock-In-Trent," he once mis-spelt it). His parents were an interracial couple who split when Slash was still young. His father, Anthony Hudson, designed album covers, notably Joni Mitchell's *Court And Spark*. His mother Ola was a costume artist. She designed David Bowie's clothing for the 1975 futuristic shocker, *The Man Who Fell To Earth*. A friend of his father's hit on the nickname Slash.

"When I was in England, I was very strange because I was the only kid with long hair. I was given lots of freedom as a kid. I grew up in a kind of rebellious hippy household. I started saying the word 'fuck' when I was like seven or eight years old, telling my parents to fuck off!

Slash is 23 today. The cake says it all.

"Ozzy Osborne is someone I can relate to," he explains. "His life is so rock 'n' roll oriented. He doesn't have anything else. That's the way I feel."

"They were always very attentive, and I don't have any problems with my family, nothing at all compared to a lot of musicians who complain about getting kicked out of the house because they grew their hair, or were told to 'Fuck off and get a job'. I never had that. I've always been pretty rebellious, to teachers, cops and the like, but my family, my childhood, that was pretty cool."

In 1976, Anthony Hudson emigrated with his son to

Hollywood. Slash, 11 years old, struggled a little in adjusting to his new life.

"When I came to LA and started school, I never really fitted in. I didn't really have a group of friends. Then, when I was 13 years old, I just thought, fuck it, and didn't worry about it anymore. Then all of a sudden everybody was cool, and I started becoming popular. It was really strange, but I didn't really care by then because I was into hanging out by myself, ditching school and practising guitar. And then, all of a sudden, I started getting lots of girlfriends.

"There was music in my house all my life. I never planned or aspired to be a musician or anything, I just loved music."

Slash got hooked on the idea of playing guitar while hanging out with a friend he'd stumbled upon at high school, Steven Adler.

"He had a guitar and an amp and he'd just plug in and turn it up all the way up and bang on it real loud. And I was just fucking fascinated with it.

"Most guitarists start playing guitar to get laid, to look cool or to get some heavy image. I started playing guitar out of ignorance, because I wanted to play an instrument that was rock 'n' roll orientated, but I didn't know back then the difference between bass and lead guitar or any of that shit! I basically chose the guitar because it had more strings!"

Right: Soundcheck, Dallas 1988. A lazy afternoon jam with Izzy, Duff and Steven.

"There was music in my house all my life. I never planned or aspired to be a musician or anything, I just loved music."

"I don't think of it as a phallic symbol. I don't think it's a symbol of anything. Basically, as far as what I use a guitar for, it's just something to hide behind, because I'm quite shy."

Softly spoken, Slash is more introverted than his whiplash guitar playing and arrogant stage demeanour suggest.

"I'm not nervous on stage. I get into being up there, it's this huge energy release. When I'm up on stage, that's my element. But I avoid eye contact. I've also got my guitar to hide behind.

"I'm completely in my own world up there. I couldn't be a lead singer, there's no way I could do that."

A guitar isn't his sole mask. There's the tangle of corkscrew hair shading his eyes; then there's the omni-present bottle of sour mash. . . .

"If I don't have a drink I sink into myself. And I like it! I like being drunk, it's fun. It's a habit I picked up when I was 12 years old. It helps me, it brings me out of my shell. I can't deal with people in a social situation when I'm sober.

"I'm usually quite a good drinker, though I admit I can get a bit obnoxious when I'm drunk sometimes. I'm one of those blackout drunks. I get so fucked up I don't remember anything. I probably give the impression of being a real asshole most of the time, but I'm not really that bad."

Slash and Jack: the best of friends.

Dallas 1988. Uncompromising as ever, Guns N' Roses ate up 10–15 minutes of a 45-minute set with a rambling blues improvisation. Here, Slash cuts loose.

"I probably give the impression of being a real asshole most of the time, but I'm not really that bad."

He is, however, prey to more serious indulgences. In the early part of 1989, Guns N' Roses were forced to quit Iron Maiden's US tour. Holed up in LA with idle hands and surplus adrenalin, Slash succumbed wholly to booze and narcotics. Alarmed at this wanton self-abuse, Alan Niven packed Slash off on a purging vacation.

The guitarist was lured to Niven's management office, ostensibly for the purpose of a press interview, and was immediately bundled on to the first available flight to Hawaii.

"All in all I can't say that it hurt me. I took vitamins for, like, eight days, didn't drink that much, got a suntan. I hadn't been out of a pair of black jeans since I was about 14! I was getting ingrowing hairs on my legs!"

Izzy reckons Slash had "really stepped off the edge". "Yeah," Slash nods, "and I didn't want to do anything that'd hurt the band, so I spent eight days in fuckin' hell!"

On another occasion, Slash was nursed through heroin withdrawal for days and nights on end by Niven and his wife. Once clean, Slash disappeared from Niven's home and wound up wasted again by the next day.

Slash invited porn star Tracy Lords to America's MTV music awards ceremony in January of 1989, but only for the hell of it. It ain't love.

"The situation with women is completely fucked up because all the girls you run into that are interested in you are usually interested because you're in a band. And that tends to be pretty, er, I don't know, pretty *low*.

"It gets a little bit lonely. There's been a real downside to all this success. I'm only just realising it. I don't go out that much. I don't have that many close friends. And what close friends I have, the time I get to see them are usually few and far between."

A life on the road is both cause and cure of Slash's loneliness.

At his new home in the Hollywood hills, its decor heavy with purple and black and hung tapestries, Slash

> "I took vitamins for, like, eight days, didn't drink that much, got a suntan. I hadn't been out of a pair of black jeans since I was about 14! I was getting ingrowing hairs on my legs!"

has just his snakes for company. He owns ten snakes (boas and pythons), some of which are almost 14 feet long. They are housed in a customised serpentarium and fed on just about anything small, furry and alive.

On a tour there's less time to be lonely. There is always a score, a bottle and a girl waiting.

"Real sex," slurred Slash the morning after the night in Dallas, "is so hard to come by. But last night was cool. We got into this great position so this chick could watch in the reflection of the wardrobe mirror as I was screwing her. Pretty good birthday . . .".

Real sex; the afterglow.

THE TRAIL OF DESTRUCTION

Within four months of the Marquee gigs, Guns N' Roses were back in Britain. In chill, rain-lashed Manchester, Axl acquired a bizarre souvenir from a Scottish fan. It was a concert ticket for a show that never was: Aerosmith at the Edinburgh Playhouse, supported by Guns N' Roses.

Aerosmith cancelled the proposed UK leg of their *Permanent Vacation* tour when their record company's marketing strategy called for further American dates. This left Guns N' Roses – and manager Alan Niven – with a high-risk dilemma. Should they wait to latch on to another big-

October 1987. Back in Britain. Balls out.

name British rock tour, or should they put their balls on the chopping block and headline their own set of dates? 'Balls out' being a way of life in Guns N' Roses, they headlined. Niven boldly booked the band into 2-3000-seat halls with only 10,000 sales of *Appetite For Destruction* to their name.

Guns N' Roses returned to Britain with the sweat still fresh from a brief US tour supporting The Cult. Axl comments: "Ian Astbury [The Cult's vocalist] came to our first show at the Marquee, the one we got such a slagging for, and liked it so much he offered us the tour! So fuck those journalists who wrote those bad things."

"Ian Astbury liked what he saw. We had a great time with The Cult. Ian spent more time in our dressing room than in his own!"

For their five UK shows, Guns N' Roses averaged ticket sales of 80 per cent of capacity. The final night at the Hammersmith Odeon fell just 200 tickets short of a sell-out.

As the band's fame escalated, so did their infamy. Axl began in earnest his habit of ripping hotel telephones out of walls. Though a neat way to rid himself of aggression, it meant that ordering meals via room service was a touch problematic. Holes in varying sizes appeared in the walls of the band's hotels. Room furniture was haphazardly re-arranged. TV repair companies boomed. Over-zealous fans came close to overturning the tour bus in the north of England.

Axl began in earnest his habit of ripping hotel telephones out of walls. Though a neat way to rid himself of aggression, it meant that ordering meals via room service was a touch problematic.

Todd Crew had roadied for Guns N' Roses for three years. Working with the band seemed to give him

something else to live for besides his heroin habit. However, back in June, Todd passed out drunk for the whole of the first Marquee show. By the time Guns N' Roses made their return to London, Todd had died from an overdose.

At Hammersmith an embittered Axl dedicated Dylan's 'Knockin' On Heaven's Door' (a song they had played for the first time in public at the Marquee) to Todd's memory.

If those five shows in October '87 lacked some of the mania of their British debut – where Slash and Duff stagedived into the Marquee crowd – they were still hard proof that Guns N' Roses' fireball charisma doesn't dissipate in bigger, colder arenas.

Having conquered as prestigious a venue as the Hammersmith Odeon, Guns N' Roses had, by the end of 1987, achieved a credibility and a status above that merited on their record sales alone.

While Aerosmith stayed rooted in their own backyard, Guns N' Roses dared and won.

Right and below: Axl on roadie Todd Crew's street-illegal hog in Los Angeles, where Todd overdosed and died.

"CAPTAIN AMERICA'S BEEN TORN APART..."

'Sweet Child O' Mine' melted the very heart of America. In the week of 10 September 1988, 'Sweet Child' became Guns N' Roses' first and (to date) only number 1 US single, helping transform *Appetite For Destruction* into one of the phenomena of 1980s rock 'n' roll.

By September of the next year, three more top 10 singles had been amassed: 'Paradise City', 'Welcome To The Jungle' and 'Patience'. Intense roadwork broke America when many predicted it would break Guns N' Roses.

"They didn't expect us to last a week!" snorts Izzy. "Touring really doesn't faze you. If you get twisted

backstage, the walk to the bus is only a few yards, y'know? But yeah, if you get twisted every night, you start draggin'."

"Touring has its downfalls," admits Slash. "It's a distorted kind of reality, but I swear to God, that 45 minutes or whatever makes it all worth it. When you're not touring you're always looking for something to fulfil that buzz."

"The thing about being on the road constantly is that you never really have any big problems hanging over you the whole time. When you're moving around from city to

"It's more addictive than any drug I could imagine," adds Izzy. "It's fucking terrible coming off the road. You come down real hard. It's like the world stops moving."

city you don't think about anything except getting to the next gig. Then when you come off the road this whole other world that's been waiting for you starts fuckin' with you. I mean, I hate having to deal with normal day-to-day shit. It leaves no time for anything else."

Guns N' Roses spent time at the beginning of 1988 headlining a tour of US theatres, but major arena supports offered great exposure. In November '87 they were invited on to Mötley Crüe's 'Girls, Girls, Girls' tour when Whitesnake quit to undertake headline shows of their own. Crüe plus Guns was hell on wheels.

Steven Adler broke a fist in a bar brawl and was replaced on a number of dates by Cinderella drummer Fred Coury, but the tour's major casualty was Crüe bass player Nikki Sixx. Sixx once lay clinically dead for a full two minutes as the result of a massive heroin overdose and was only saved by paramedics kickstarting his heart

Below: Dallas. Axl exchanges his hat for one which Duff begged off photographer Ian T. Tilton.

with shots of adrenalin. The Crüe's tour was cut short when Sixx retired "exhausted." Guns, meanwhile, raged on.

In May Guns N' Roses joined the start of Iron Maiden's North American tour in Canada but pulled out as the dates wound down the West Coast towards LA. Axl's voice was shot from too much of a good time on the road.

By 15 July, when Guns began supporting Aerosmith, Axl's self-discipline had strengthened. He denied himself booze and remained hidden away behind his hotel room door while Izzy, Slash, Steve and Duff blitzed every club and bar under the night stars. Axl would often appear just 20 minutes before a show and psyche himself up to a loud playback of Queensrÿche's 'The Needle Lies'.

Explains Slash: "You gotta understand that with this bunch, excess is best an' all that shit. Axl knows he has to keep from smoking or drinking or doing drugs to maintain his voice. He doesn't hang out that much because the atmosphere that's created by the other four members of this band is pretty, uh . . ."

"Conducive to deterioration," Izzy smiles.

"He just hangs out by himself. He takes it all pretty seriously. I couldn't do it," Slash confesses. "He's doing well to maintain a certain sanity level seeing as he can't go out 'cos of his position in the band. If he was doing what we were doing he wouldn't be able to sing at all!

"The Aerosmith tour was the first *rock 'n' roll* tour we've done. The Mötley tour was fun, but the vibe between us and Aerosmith was great.

"Those guys are around their 30s and 40s, they've been through a lotta shit and we have a lotta respect for them. We grew up listening to their music; this and the Stones and AC/DC, that's what sorta formed what we are. That's the only way you get any kinda personality – through influences."

On that tour, guitarist Joe Perry's Toxic Twins T-shirt was Aerosmith's only throwback to their mid-'70s chemical haze." Clean, detoxed, Aerosmith had hung up their wild years. Guns N' Roses' were only just beginning. . . .

On and offstage in Dallas. Tour manager, and now co-manager, Doug Goldstein blows a raspberry, sort of.

While Slash chugged bourbon between songs, Perry, a good 15 years his senior, swigged from a bottle of mineral water.

"It's funny," grins Slash. "They like to talk about drugs. They don't *do* drugs, they just like to talk about them, it's cool to be around that."

"You drag your ass into the gig sometimes," laughs Izzy, "and you

Starplex Arena, Dallas, Texas.
24 July 1988.

see those guys and you think, Awww, fuck!"

"They're eating watermelon and drinking tea," Slash continues, incredulous. "They love to ask you about what you did last night and how fucked up you got. They go, man, I've been up since nine o'clock this morning, and you say, What drugs are you doing? They say, No, I just been up since nine!

"When we got to LA it was a gas. We did 'Mama Kin' together. It was nice, too, because we were told by the people that worked for them that they would never go to the side of the stage and watch any of the bands that opened for them usually. But for us they were there just about every night. The first time I looked over and saw them all standing there watching us play, that fucked with me, it was weird.

"I did a guitar solo one night – one of those finger-pickin' slow blues things – and after the show, Steven Tyler [Aerosmith vocalist] got me to one side and said, 'That was amazing!' I just stood there and said, 'Well, thanks,' and couldn't think of anything else to say. I was blown away. That's something I'll never forget."

By September and the tour's end countless cigarettes and at least a fifth of Jack Daniel's per day had turned Slash's tongue a disgusting brown-black. Yet, incredibly, Guns N' Roses had survived their two-year sex, drugs 'n' rock 'n' roll marathon. They even pulled through a crazy mid-tour crisis that left the band minus a singer for three days.

In February 1988 Axl didn't show up for a gig in Phoenix, Arizona. When he did appear the following day, the rest of the band, angered and disappointed, told Axl he was out of Guns N' Roses. The bitterness lasted for three tense days before Slash and Izzy met with Axl and heard out the singer's reasons for missing the Phoenix show. They quit bitchin' and made up, but the hurt lingers even now.

Above: **Steven Tyler of Aerosmith. Dallas 1988. The Aerosmith/ Guns N' Roses American tour was dubbed The Greatest Rock 'N' Roll Double Bill ever seen.**

"That's been one of the stories that's gotten bigger than all of us," sighs Slash. "And as little as it was, it's past tense and it's not worth talking about 'cos it doesn't relate to what's going on now."

Guns N' Roses do not swallow their pride too often, but on this one occasion, a little humility saved them.

By September and the tour's end countless cigarettes and at least a fifth of Jack Daniel's per day had turned Slash's tongue a disgusting brown-black.

Below: Steven runs up one hell of a tab in a Dallas beerhole. Matching him drink for drink is Dave 'Jr' Elefson of Megadeth.

DUFF McKAGAN

Duff McKagan isn't the quiet man of Guns N' Roses. Nor is he the wild one. He's more the tall cool one; a little crazy but dependable, fun but rarely hysterical.

Born Michael McKagan in Seattle, Washington, 5 February 1965, Duff "grew up surrounded by music. They always played the rock stations in my house when I was a kid."

Duff was the youngest of eight chidren, most of whom were involved with local bands at some stage. Even his father had a love of music, singing harmonies in a barbershop quartet. It was Duff's brother, Bruce, who introduced him to the bass guitar.

"When I was in eighth grade Bruce gave me lessons and I just got right into it."

Between ages 15 and 19 Duff drifted in and out of 31 Seattle bands, shifting from bass to drums and on to guitar.

> "I started out as a bassist and then a local band spotted me fucking around on drums and asked me to join 'em."

Duff was even offered a gig with UK punk brats The Angelic Upstarts.

"The band came to the States years ago with a guy called Andy Thompson on drums, but he wasn't working out. Anyway, they crashed at the house of a friend of mine while they were in Seattle, so I got to know them. At the time I was playing drums, and out of the blue one day they called me from San Francisco, said they were looking for a new drummer and asked if I'd be interested.

"I rehearsed with 'em, but they wanted me to move to England and I was shit scared of making such a jump. I turned 'em down and stayed with the band I was with at the time. I thought I'd made a wise choice, but that group disappeared without trace."

Aged 21, Duff tired of the Seattle club treadmill and decided to try his luck in LA. Then a guitar player, he chose to revert to the bass to help stack the odds a little more in his favour.

"I had heard the stories about LA, where there were millions of guitar players, and I really didn't think I was good enough to be one of the top players. So in order to get my foot in the door, I decided to get a bass and a bass amp and go down to LA!"

Duff played in just two LA bands. The first was Road

Duff McKagan. The coolest head in Guns N' Roses.

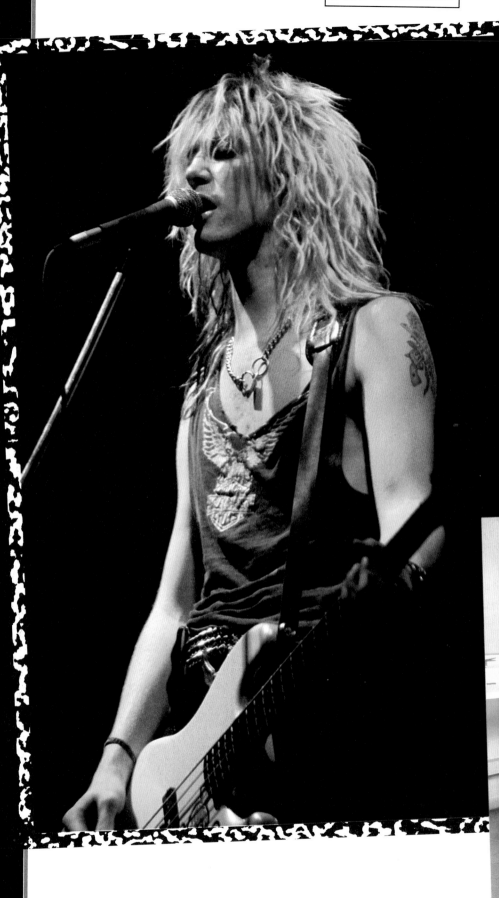

Guns N' Roses
vodka-swillin' token
cowboy, on stage
and in the dentist's
chair.

Crew, where he first encountered Slash and Steven but walked out on them when gigs, and even rehearsals, dried up. The second was Guns N' Roses. . . .

Duff was the first member of Guns N' Roses to marry, in May of 1988. The band was already booked to play shows in Canada with Iron Maiden but the wedding received the official go ahead when a temporary replacement for Duff was found, namely Haggis, ex of The Cult and a friend of Guns N' Roses. They and Haggis had played on the same bill when the bassist was still a part of UK cock-rocker Zodiac Mindwarp's Love Reaction. Duff's bride was Mandy Brix, singer with LA band The Lame Flames.

"She's in a band," Duff winks, "so she understands life on the road."

As Izzy once remarked, "Duff loves his vodka" – the fifth bottle of Russian Stolichnaya on the band's backstage rider is his – yet he remains the most "even-keeled" of the five. He's the first one to pick up a football and fool around with the crew.

On tour, Duff works out each day with weights. In addition, he completes running exercises up flights of stairs. At home in Los Angeles, he has a mountain bike on which he covers 30 miles per day of hilly terrain.

"I've gotten into three fights recently with guys just trying to show off to their girlfriends. I won all of 'em, though," he grins. "I ride that bike constantly, so I'm in good shape."

This also helps Duff stand up to all that Stoli. He and Slash, Guns N' Roses' alcohol-poisoning club, checked into a Japanese hotel as 'The Likesheet Brothers – Phil and Luke.' When Duff mixes his guests a vodka and orange, he adds barely enough juice to colour the spirit, let alone flavour it.

Along with Slash, Duff handles around 90 per cent of publicity chores once the band's up and rolling on tour. And, at the end of a tour road-fever exacts its toll on Duff's appearance. There are few sights in rock 'n' roll to compare with Duff McKagan in a CBGB's vest, sweatpants cut off at the thigh, bare knees, snakeskin boots and a tacky stetson.

"This song," chokes Axl from a stage in Texas, "features Duff McKagan – our token cowboy – on bass."

The crowd, of course, loves him.

"I've gotten into three fights recently with guys just trying to show off to their girlfriends. I won all of 'em, though," he grins. "I ride that bike constantly, so I'm in good shape."

There are few sights in rock 'n' roll to compare with Duff McKagan in a CBGB's vest, sweatpants cut off at the thigh, bare knees, snakeskin boots and a tacky stetson.

PUBLIC ENEMIES AT NUMBER ONE

August 1988 was a bittersweet month for Guns N' Roses. When they arrived in England, via Concorde, for an appearance at the annual Monster Of Rock festival at Castle Donington, *Appetite For Destruction* had just hit the number one position in the US albums listings, ousting Tracy Chapman's eponymous debut.

Peaking 13 months after its release, *Appetite* was an unlikely number one; unapologetically loud, foul-mouthed and bloody-nosed, raw and glaring like a fresh tattoo burnt into tender new skin.

"I think the only reason it could possibly have gone to number one is because we're filling some sort of void," argues Slash. "It's not because the songs are all huge hits – that's the last thing they are. They're just a bunch of dirty rock 'n' roll songs. So I figure we're just the resident down-and-dirty rock band in town at the moment. Everybody wants to have that record because it's not really that safe . . . and it looks cool next to the George Michael records in their collection."

A number one record was perhaps the ultimate triumph of Guns N' Roses' integrity, but the euphoria wasn't to last. A huge crowd of 107,000 rock fans squeezed into the Donington site on August 30. Two never made it out alive. They were lost in the crush at the front of the stage, trampled and suffocated in Donington's thick red mud. Guns N' Roses were on stage as they died.

The Guns were unaware of the

> "So I figure we're just the resident down-and-dirty rock band in town at the moment. Everybody wants to have that record because it's not really that safe . . . and it looks cool next to the George Michael records in their collection."

Opposite: Donington Park, August 1988.

Axl at Donington.

Donington 1988. Triumph before tragedy.

fatalities until they returned to their hotel in Leicester late in the afternoon. However, sensing panic and danger in the crowd (provoked by the collapse of a giant video screen at one side of the stage), they had attempted to calm the pushing, shoving mass with a concentration of slower songs. 'Patience' and 'Sweet Child O' Mine' ended their set. Axl left the stage with words that would take on a grim irony: "Don't kill yourselves."

"I don't know really what to think about it," Axl admitted later. "I don't want anybody to get hurt. We want the exact opposite."

"We didn't tell people to smash each other. We didn't tell people, 'Drink so much alcohol that you can't fucking stand up.' I don't feel responsible in those ways."

Slash adds: "When things started getting out of hand we had to stop the set to get those kids out of the crowd. We *had* to stop. I remember looking down into the crowd at the front of the stage thinking, 'Oh fuck!' When we were back at the hotel Alan [Niven] told me what had happened and I couldn't believe it. I've thought about it a lot since then, though, and I've decided I can't take personal responsibility for what happened at Donington. The way I see it, it was too many people pushing up to the stage.

"What really bums me out the most, though, the thing that really pisses me off, is the thought that somebody was standing on top of somebody else, and didn't care, or was too selfish or too self-involved to care. You can't stand on somebody and not know they're there. It's sick.

"There's been a couple of gigs where we've consciously had to slow down a gear. Donington, of course, was one of them. There was another gig, in upstate New York on the Aerosmith tour, which was particularly intense too. After we got off stage, the medics' booth outside was just loaded with kids."

Guns N' Roses have pushed crowds to the brink of chaos, but, as the Donington tragedies proved, the madness must end somewhere. In Saratoga Springs, New York, "there was nearly a riot," admits Izzy. "I get off on that kind of vibe, where anything's just about ready to crack. When there's 25,000 people and they have, like, three security guys. God, it was intense, man. It was just on that fucking edge of 25,000 people coming down on the stage."

"At times, like in Philly," reckons Axl, "I think I could've easily started a riot. It's great watching 'em go crazy but I don't want to see people get hurt."

"I'd been wondering whether we should write something to the parents of those kids who died at Donington," reveals Slash. "But then I thought that nothing which comes from us was gonna be that much of a statement to make to those people anyway. They don't want to read some shit from some simple-minded rock band who the parents haven't even heard of but were responsible, as far as they're concerned, for the demise of their children. So in the end I decided to leave it alone."

"I actually don't know if the acci-

> "At times, like in Philly," reckons Axl, "I think I could've easily started a riot. It's great watching 'em go crazy but I don't want to see people get hurt."

dent was our fault or not," shrugs Duff. "If someone were to ask me face-to-face whether Guns N' Roses were to blame, I couldn't say with any conviction that we're not. I don't think we can be held responsible, but maybe we have to take some of the blame. After all, we were on stage when those kids died, and had Guns N' Roses not existed then perhaps the tragedy wouldn't have occurred.

"It weighs very heavily on us and whatever anyone else may write or say about the incident can't make us feel any worse. Quite honestly, we couldn't give a fuck about the media trying to make us the scapegoats. That thing will haunt me forever anyway. It's strange, but tragedy and pain do seem to dog our career."

Slash displays
his style at
Donington.

"That thing will haunt me forever anyway. It's strange, but tragedy and pain do seem to dog our career."

"We don't go out of our way to look for trouble," insists Slash, "but the slightest incident takes on un-believable proportions. We cause some chaos, because we think that's what rock 'n' roll is all about. Most groups are happy to do as they're told in order to be commercial and suc-ceed, even give up their identity. We never wanted to do that.

"That's why we're the new public enemy number one, and every sheriff and cop wants just one thing, to nail one of Guns N' Roses."

"That's why we're the new public enemy number one, and every sheriff and cop wants just one thing, to nail one of Guns N' Roses."

Above: Security staff pull one fan to safety from the Donington crush.

Below: Slash backstage at Donington with Jeff Young (then of Megadeth), Lars Ulrich of Metallica and Dave Mustaine of Megadeth.

IZZY STRADLIN'

Where Axl possesses "a natural ability to attract attention, much of it negative", Izzy Stradlin' has the ability to be "invisible". Izzy can slip unnoticed from a room. Cool, languid, he's perhaps the most withdrawn of the five no-goods who make up Guns N' Roses and has experienced some difficulty in coming to terms with life as "a Beatle".

The other four band members have all bought properties with their royalty earnings. Izzy has spent comparatively little of his money. He's bought a car, but no home. Indecisive, living on his nerves, Izzy has hoarded.

He was born plain Jeff Isabelle in "Bumfuck" (read 'Lafayette'), Indiana, 8 April 1962.

"The fact that I'm from Indiana," he spits, "has no business being in my career! It's a worthless fucking place."

Izzy and Axl go back to their early teens. Izzy's always been cooler, quieter, though no less intense. Axl has the blacker police record but Izzy has survived the "toxic hell' of hardened drug addiction, just as Axl got out while he could. Though introverted, Izzy is resilient. In the words of Guns N' Roses old LA flyposters: 'Only the strong survive.'

As the only member of the band to graduate from college with a degree, Izzy can't be typecast as the untameable rock rebel illiterate. He's happiest with a bottle of Valpolicella and a Rolling Stones album. On Guns N' Roses' first visit to London in the summer of '87 he blew a bunch of per diems on a couple of Stones tapes, *Some Girls* and *Sticky Fingers*, which he required as inspiration right there and then.

Izzy has been likened to Keith Richards on many occasions. This is fine as regards great rhythm guitar playing, but isn't he concerned that this reckless rock 'n' roll life will leave him looking like Keef warmed up inside 15 years?

"I think Keith's held up pretty well!" Izzy laughs.

Duff, Slash and Steven generally like to hit the black-top soon after a show and roll into the next town in good

As the only member of the band to graduate from college with a degree, Izzy can't be typecast as the untameable rock rebel illiterate. He's happiest with a bottle of Valpolicella and a Rolling Stones album.

Izzy relaxes with a guitar, a bottle and a girl.

Right: Soundcheck (left) and the show proper (right). Dallas 1988.

time for their day off. Travelling on a separate tourbus, Izzy and Axl prefer to linger, to go into the city and socialize.

Early press coverage created a different image of Izzy, depicting him as cheerless and acidic, Guns N' Roses' "resident cynic."

His brutal retorts ("What's the bullshit with the ages?", "Seattle? No-one's from Seattle", "Fuck you and your magazine!") were more than simple bloody-minded invective. Izzy demonstrated his impatience with dull questions by exploiting the sharp end of his dry humour.

He's not above toilet humour either. On one hot, lazy afternoon in America's South, Izzy couldn't get British photographer Ian Tilton into the tourbus shit-house quick enough. "Hey, Ian, get a load of this!" An emotional Izzy had just laid the longest turd of his life and made sure that the coiled monster was immortalized on film.

Izzy Stradlin' is the most independent of Guns N' Roses. All he asks of road manager (and now co-manager) Doug Goldstein is to be left to himself.

Privacy is sanity and Izzy will often just take off alone in a hired car. No girlfriend, just him and his thoughts.

"I don't think drugs or anything else is as important to anybody in that band as being in Guns N' Roses is," said country/rock singer Steve Earle, a friend of the band.

Earle's right. Izzy's still around.

W. AXL ROSE ATE MY POODLE

Shocking fans and critics alike, Guns N' Roses turned the 'new Aerosmith' mantle on its head with the release in November '88 of *GN'R Lies*.

Originally titled 'The Sex, The Drugs, The Violence: The Shocking Trust', *Lies* coupled *Live ?!*@ Like A Suicide* (re-released by public demand; secondhand copies of the initial pressing had been selling for more than $100) with four new cuts that owed more to the Rolling Stones than to Aerosmith.

The sleeve of *GN'R Lies* parodied the tabloid newspapers that had warned Britain of the imminent arrival of "dog-killing rockers" Guns N' Roses back in 1987. "The artwork," remarked Slash during his vodka binge of '88 (sick of 'Jack', he was sinking "around three litres of vodka per day"), "is a sorta *Sunday Sport* or *Sun* kinda vibe, with a Page Three girl on it. We did this EP for the same reason as we first did *Live ?!*@ Like A Suicide*. It's material that we wanted off our chests but without taking up too much space."

Commenting on the rough nature of the EP's mix, he added: "It's real simple, real sloppy. You can hear us talking, there's guitar picks dropping. Real off-the-cuff."

"Half-assed" Duff calls it, but the songs are great and the performances honest and electric. "Half-assed" or not, *GN'R Lies* joined *Appetite For Destruction* in the US top 10 in February of '89 and has sold in excess of two million copies in America alone.

'Patience' had been worked into shape on the Aerosmith dates and as a single made the charts in both Britain and the USA. Reminiscent of the Stones' 'Dead Flowers', 'Used To Love Her' is, says Izzy, "a joke. Wife beating's been around for 10 million years or something. I mean," he laughs, quoting American sledgehammer comedian Sam Kinison, "I don't advocate it. I *understand* it. But I don't treat women any differently than I treat men."

"If some guy goes out an' kills his girlfriend," says Slash, "that's gonna fuck my head up. I mean, this is serious. It's affecting the lives of people you don't even know, which is definitely a scary thing, to have that much power. The version of 'You're Crazy' is slow, mid-tempo, sorta half-time of what's on *Appetite*. It's a lot bluesier. That's the way me 'n' Axl 'n' Izzy originally wrote it, on an acoustic. Then we went into rehearsals for the album. I had a huge Marshall stack and my Les Paul and we

"If some guy goes out an' kills his girlfriend," says Slash, "that's gonna fuck my head up. I mean, this is serious."

just doubled it up right away and turned it into a real fast song."

It was 'One In A Million', however, which created the ugly controversy promised by *Lies*' tacky sleeve. Originally titled 'Police And Niggers', 'One In A Million' is a brutal recounting of Axl's early years in Hollywood. It isn't pretty.

"I went back and forth from Indiana eight times in my first year in Hollywood," Axl recalls. "I wrote that song about being dropped off at the bus station and everything that was going on. The black dudes trying to sell you drugs is where the line 'Police and niggers, get out of my way' comes from. I've seen these

**1988. Trouble here
trouble there**

huge black dudes pull Bowie knives on people for their boom boxes [ghetto blasters] and shit. It's ugly.

"When I say I'm a smalltown white boy I'm just saying I'm no better than anyone else I've described. I'm just trying to get through life, that's all."

'One In A Million' aims some low punches – "Immigrants and faggots, they make no sense to me/They come to our country, and think they'll do as they please" – but Slash reckons the outrage provoked by the song hinges on a single word.

"You have to watch this shit, you say. 'Police and niggers' was a line I really didn't want Axl to sing, but, y'know, Axl's the kind of person who will sing whatever it is he feels like singing. What that line was supposed to mean was 'niggers' in the sense of the sort of street thugs that you run into in LA. Especially if you're a Midwestern, naive young kid just coming into the city for the first time, and there's these guys trying to pawn this on you and push this on you. It's a heavily intimidat- ing kind of thing for someone like that. I've been living in Hollywood so long, I'm used to it."

Yet while respecting Axl's right to freedom of expression, Slash can't help being disappointed that a "great track" has been spoilt, or at least overshadowed, by controversy.

"It bothers me because I'm part black and I don't have anything against black individuals at all. And what else bothers me is that one of the nice things about Guns N' Roses is that we've always been a people's band, and we've never really segregated our fans. And then with the release of that song, I think it did something that wasn't necessarily positive for the band. Personally, I don't think that statement should have been made. I talked to my mom – who lives in Europe – for the first time in ages and I asked her on the

> "And what else bothers me is that one of the nice things about Guns N' Roses is that we've always been a people's band, and we've never really segregated our fans."

phone if she'd heard the EP yet, and she told me no, right?

"But my little brother was out there with her, and when he came back he told me, yeah, she actually had heard it, but she was so shocked that we'd said something like that, she didn't know what to say to me about it."

"If we offended anyone," says Slash, "it wasn't intentional."

Ultimately, the controversy will cool and die and *GN'R Lies* will be regarded as great rock 'n' roll, pure and simple. Izzy and Alan Niven

believe it might have been greater still. They argued that the original sessions, cut in early '87, "kicked shit" out of the 1988 recordings. Axl, however, was unhappy with his performance from '87, so the latter tapes eventually made it into the record stores. One song from the lost *Lies* sessions, the lewd 'Corn Chucker' (just look at an ear of corn, they smile), may well surface on GN'R's projected X-rated EP (in addition, punk songs by Fear, Misfits, Sex Pistols and Adolescents are likely to constitute yet another EP).

"The *Lies* EP is another aspect of our abilities," says Axl. "We can only put so many songs on one album, and we wanted *Appetite For Destruction* to be a full hard rock record from beginning to end. The reason we released the EP was so that we don't get pigeonholed into one type of music that people expect from us. We like all kinds of music and we'll play all types of music.

> "When I say I'm a smalltown white boy I'm just saying I'm no better than anyone else I've described. I'm just trying to get through life, that's all."

> "We have pieces of everything in our band. You don't see a lot of that any more. Queen used to do it, and Zeppelin, but nowadays people tend to stay in one vein. Play whatever the fuck you want to play. That's what we've done."

"DON'T POINT YOUR FINGER AT ME"

Controversy sticks to Guns N' Roses like a shadow. 'One In A Million' was a storm in a thousand (ironically, it was the word "faggots" and not "niggers" which sparked a fury over the song and resulted in Guns N' Roses being banned from appearing at an AIDS benefit show in New York in the summer of '89).

It all began with horror tales of substance abuse. For early LA shows, Guns N' Roses' billing read 'fresh from detox'. Smack, sex, booze, tattoos – their craving for excess sucked on the '70s but reeked of danger.

When rock's newest miscreants made for London and the Marquee Club, British families locked up both their daughters and their dogs, lest these canine-killin' crazies felt the uncontrollable urge to rub out a few more little critters. In fact, Axl had merely joked about slaying poodles. He did shoot a pig in LA one night in 1989 with a single bullet between the eyes, but only for a barbecue.

British families locked up both their daughters and their dogs, lest these canine-killin' crazies felt the uncontrollable urge to rub out a few more little critters.

He did shoot a pig in LA one night in 1989 with a single bullet between the eyes, but only for a barbecue.

Backstage at the Starplex, Dallas, 1988. There are 15 minutes till showtime.

Further British public outcry greeted the release of *Appetite For Destruction* in its original sleeve; the Robert Williams painting depicted a robot which had raped a girl and now faced annihilation by some sabre-toothed vision from hell. A number of major retail chains – W.H. Smith among them – refused to stock the record until the cover was re-designed.

"I submitted the *Appetite* cover as a joke," says Axl, "'cause I didn't think anyone would use it. I just really liked it and tossed it in, and everybody else flipped! I couldn't believe they really wanted to use it."

Allegations of sadistic sexism were rejected by the band. Williams, they

argued, was portraying the rape of its people by a savage society.

The lyrics of *Appetite* were branded "irresponsible". Slash comments on 'Mr Brownstone' and its discourse on heroin: "We never said it was cool, but if kids misunderstood it then that fucks me up. I don't want to be a part of fucking up kids' lives."

Radio wouldn't touch the first UK single. Peppered with obscenities, 'It's So Easy' was one of the great punk songs of the 1980s.

At Donington in '88, Guns N' Roses did all in their power to quell the chaos. They were blameless, but those two deaths put the band's comments on crowd violence into a cold new perspective.

Fistfights, riots, arrests, fines; controversy has raged at virtually every roadstop Guns N' Roses have made.

When they toured Australia in December of '88, the local authorities mistakenly felt that Axl's preamble to 'Mr Brownstone' condoned and glorified drug misuse; this was deemed a public offence and a warrant for Axl's arrest was issued. Police staked out the band's hotel but they had already hot-footed it to New

Zealand. Following their gig in Auckland, Guns N' Roses' home journey was re-routed to avoid Australia, where the police warrants were presumably still valid.

Trouble in Australia was fated: only three months before those dates, GN'R ran up a feud with those darlings of Australian rock, INXS. INXS were headlining a show at Dallas's huge Texas Stadium, with Guns N' Roses second on the bill.

By their own admission, Guns played a lousy show. They hadn't carried out a soundcheck.

As he left the stage, Axl upheld the great Texan ethic of 'biggest is best'; naturally enough, when INXS' name came up, the insulted flowed from there.

Slash and Axl: toxic twins.

Straight-talking, opinionated, Axl won't bite his lip, back off or sweeten his tongue. His are brutal words, but then, like Slayer or Metallica, Guns N' Roses are "a brutal band for brutal times."

WE'RE DOIN'
WHAT WE WANNA
AND WE'RE PULLING IT OFF

"Rock 'n' roll in general has just sucked a big fucking dick since the Pistols," snarls Izzy.

"I hope we've re-introduced the idea of being natural, of being for real and adopting a down-to-earth approach," says Slash. "We want to put integrity back into music. What this industry's about these days is pretty obvious – trying to polish everything up. Everything's like technopop, even heavy metal stuff.

"We go against every standard of this industry. Even when we play live – we're like a club band when we play to, like, 20,000 people. We do whatever we feel like doing."

"It's really weird having such success," adds Duff. "People tell me how great we are and I think to myself, 'We haven't done anything yet'! All this band has done so far is put out one LP and a half-assed mini-album. I often wonder if we deserve what's happened to us. Still, we did tour forever and certainly paid our dues."

Guns N' Roses kicked the shit out of the music industry. Only Tracy

Guns N' Roses connect with to-day's youth simply because some-thing of the kid still kicks inside

Chapman and Metallica have done likewise within the past decade.

Guns N' Roses reclaimed rock 'n' roll from the old and the weak. Their music draws on past eras but, hardened by a contemporary cynicism, the band don't cling to icons out of sentimental respect.

Izzy described a Rod Stewart show with a smile as "relaxing, like a quaalude." "I love Jimmy Page," sighed Slash while contemplating Page's LA Forum Show of 1988, "but he bores the fuck outta me sometimes!"

"Mick Jagger," he sneers, "should have died after *Some Girls*, when he was still cool."

them. On the Aerosmith trail in '88, tour manager Doug Goldstein went for an early morning round of golf on the course at the band's hotel and met with the sight of Duff, Slash and Steven – each huddled in his own motorised golf cart – racing the wrong way up the fairway and looking like rock's own Banana Splits!

What next for the definitive rock 'n' roll band of the age?

"We have a lot of stuff written," says Axl. "There are probably 30 songs to choose from already. We have about 10 ballads that I feel are more credible than 'Sweet Child O' Mine'."

'November Rain', which is eight minutes long, is among them.

"We wanted to save those ballads, because we wanted to wait until we had a bigger audience. We never imagined it would be this big, but we have some songs which we've been waiting to spring on people for a long time."

One off-the-wall number that is scheduled for inclusion on the new record is the rap song which Guns N' Roses played for two weeks on the Iron Maiden tour before Axl's voice gave in.

"Other than that, we're going to try and make the longest record that we can. We're going to try and put down as many songs as we can. I don't know if it will be a very, very long single album or maybe a double album."

"Rock 'n' roll is based on attitude," asserts Slash.

"We want to tour, travel, continue the big Guns N' Roses adventure," says Axl. "And indulge ourselves. And fuck a lot! Drug use is not in the past. We scare the shit out of each other because we don't want to lose what we have as a family."

"This band is so realistic in what we do and what we play. We never said we were the best rock 'n' roll band in the world so don't judge us as that. We just go out and play."

It's Axl who has recently held Guns N' Roses together. The pressures of a hard and fast rock 'n' roll lifestyle had begun to tell as the band played four shows at the Los Angeles Coliseum as support to the re-

animated Rolling Stones. Early reports said that Axl had wigged out, that before the show he'd driven to the backstage area at the wheel of an LAPD squad car, siren wailing. And that he'd announced from the stage that he was quitting Guns N' Roses because too many of the band were "dancing with Mr Brownstone."

The last of these rumours bears the seed of truth. Axl was desperate to shake Slash, Izzy and Steven out of drugged stupors and felt the only way he'd do it was to threaten to quit the band. It worked.

On the second night Axl told the crowd there'd be no split. Slash said his piece on the perils of narcotics. He and Izzy and Steven cleaned up. Guns N' Roses survived.

"There *is* a self-destructive element about this band," concludes Slash, "but the will to survive is infinitely stronger – about twice as strong – and that will ensure we're gonna be around for some time to come."